HOW TO LEAD

Children's Liturgy of the Word

Pat Fosarelli

Donna Eschenauer

Paul Turner

LITURGY
TRAINING
PUBLICATIONS

Nihil Obstat
Very Reverend Daniel A. Smilanic, JCD
Vicar for Canonical Services
Archdiocese of Chicago
March 10, 2014

Imprimatur
Most Reverend Francis J. Kane, DD
Vicar General
Archdiocese of Chicago
March 10, 2014

Authors: Pat Fosarelli, Donna Eschenauer, and Paul Turner.

Additional written material contributed by Jennifer Kerr Breedlove, Joseph DeGrocco, Maureen A. Kelly, Peter Mazar, Virginia Meager, Robert W. Piercy, Jr., Kenneth A. Riley, Kristopher W. Seaman, and Dennis Smolarski. "Writing the Prayer of the Faithful" was written by Robert W. Piercy, Jr.

Contents

People were bringing even infants to him that he might touch them, and when the disciples saw this, they rebuked them. Jesus, however, called the children to himself and said, "Let the children come to me and do not prevent them; for the kingdom of God belongs to such as these. Amen, I say to you, whoever does not accept the kingdom of God like a child will not enter it."

Luke 18:15–17

Welcome to the Ministry

Many children learn to pray as easily as they learn to eat. They naturally wonder at the world around them. Their minds fill with questions. They talk to God as they talk to friends, with honesty and love, in joy and in need. Children worship very well—if someone would just show them the way.

You are serving the Church as a leader of the Liturgy of the Word with children. In doing so, you are expanding the range of a child's abilities to pray. To perform this service, you need a living faith supported by regular prayer. Because you have experienced the presence of God, you can invite children to do the same.

There are many kinds of prayer, but this ministry specifically demands a love for liturgical prayer. Because Sunday Mass is already the cornerstone of your spiritual life, you are familiar with the power of the liturgy to form individuals and a community of faith. At Mass the community gathers on Sunday to proclaim its faith in the Resurrection. At Mass we give thanks to God and share the sacrament of the Eucharist. At Mass we hear and heed God's Word. To be an effective leader of the Liturgy of the Word with children, you need a love for Sunday Mass.

You also need a love for children. You gain insight at their words, you delight to see them play, and you melt at the love they offer you. Who doesn't love children?

The Catholic Church calls the family the foundation of society. Our *Catechism* teaches us that "[t]he family is the *original cell of social life*. It is the natural society in which husband and wife are called to give themselves in love and in the gift of life. . . . The family is the community in which, from childhood, one can learn moral values, begin to honor God, and make good use of freedom" (*Catechism of the Catholic Church* [CCC], 2207).

When you help children honor God, you help families. You help society. And you help the Church. May God reward you for your gift of service.

Children's Liturgy of the Word is a prayer service that may take place during Mass at the same time that the rest of the community celebrates its Liturgy of the Word. This children's service may take place on weekdays, but more commonly it is offered on Sundays.

Everyone gathers inside the church for the Introductory Rites. Then, just after the priest prays the Collect, the community divides. The priest invites the children to go to a different place for a Liturgy of the Word designed for their comprehension (see "Introduction," *Lectionary for Masses with Children* [LMC], 8). They may hear Scriptures from the standard *Lectionary for Mass* or from the *Lectionary for Masses with Children*, a book based on the same readings proclaimed to the rest of the community. The children return to the full assembly in time for the Preparation of the Gifts. The shape of what children experience should imitate a normal Liturgy of the Word at Mass (see LMC, 53).

The children will need someone to lead them through this time of prayer and proclamation. They need you.

The name of this activity is children's Liturgy of the Word—not children's catechesis based on the Word. The distinction is important. Certainly some catechesis may happen, as it may during Sunday Mass. But this event is structured differently from a catechetical session. It's not a a religion class or relgious education. It's not CCD (Confraternity of Christian Doctrine). It's not PSR (Parish School of Religion). It is not CGS (Catechesis of the Good Shepherd). It's not Bible study. It's not a snack break. It's prayer.

To be specific, it's liturgical prayer. It is a Liturgy of the Word happening in tandem with the one in church.

Wherever you go with the children—whether it's a chapel, a classroom, or a gym—it should feel like a place where people worship. When children arrive there, they should have a sense that they have come to pray.

Therefore, elements of liturgical prayer should be evident. The *Lectionary for Masses with Children*, or standard *Lectionary for Mass,* should occupy a central place. Someone should proclaim the readings from either of these books. Music may include the Responsorial Psalm and the Gospel Acclamation, and even some other song inspired by the readings of the day.

You will be sharing your thoughts about the readings. Here you may follow good catechetical principles. But overall, the children should experience ritual —silence and song, hearing and proclaiming, processions and reverence for the Word of God.

That reverence is one of the greatest gifts you can share with children. The *General Instruction of the Roman Missal* (GIRM) says, "When the Sacred Scriptures are read in the Church, God himself speaks to his people, and Christ, present in his word, proclaims the Gospel. Therefore, the readings from the Word of God are to be listened to reverently by everyone, for they are an element of the greatest importance in the Liturgy" (GIRM, 29).

Think about that. As the readings are proclaimed, God is speaking. As the Gospel is proclaimed. Christ is speaking. Readers use their own voices, but the words are all coming from God.

That is why attentive listening is so critical during the proclamation of the Scriptures. Children learn to listen when parents and teachers are speaking. They can also learn to listen when God is speaking.

The Second Vatican Council said that Christ is present during the Mass in different ways. For example, he is present "especially under the Eucharistic elements." And, pertinent to your ministry, "he is present in his word, since it is he himself who speaks when the holy Scriptures are read in the Church" (*Constitution on the Sacred Liturgy* [CSL], 7).

This message may appeal to children who are preparing for their first Holy Communion. They do not yet open their mouths to share in the sacrament of the Eucharist, but they are sharing in the presence of Christ every time they open their ears to receive his Word. To help these children encounter Christ, the Church lets them hear his Word at their level of understanding.

The Gospel according to John opens with a glorious meditation on the Word. God's Word was present in the beginning, and that Word became flesh in Jesus Christ. When we are proclaiming and hearing God's Word, we come in touch with this great mystery: It is in God's very nature to communicate with us.

This book will help you hear God's Word and share it with children. As you do, give thanks to the God who made you, speaks to you, and relies on you to tell children the Good News.

—Paul Turner

The Purpose and History of the Liturgy of the Word with Children

In the Scriptures, God speaks to us. At Mass, God speaks to a particular people gathered at a particular time in a particular place. The Word will affect us in different ways. Each person will hear the message uniquely, as the Holy Spirit reaches into the hearts of us all to place within them the message that comes from God. When a parish celebrates a separate Liturgy of the Word with children, the vision is first and foremost that children will be led to "full, conscious, and active participation" in the liturgy (CSL, 14).

The goal for a separate Liturgy of the Word with children is to help them hear God's message in a way that they can participate. The most important point for genuinely understanding the vision for celebrating the Liturgy of the Word with children is that it is *liturgy*—the ritual prayer of the Church—and not classroom instruction. This is not to say that it does not catechize. Liturgy and catechesis are intimately connected. They are two sides of the same coin. For centuries, the Homily was the principal form of catechesis for the Church. The Church's document on catechesis, *General Directory for Catechesis* (GDC), tells us that liturgy must be regarded as an "eminent kind of catechesis" (71; referencing CT, 23; cf. SC, 35 ad 3; CIC, 777, 1 and 2). and that liturgy educates us to active participation, contemplation, and silence.

> [The] full and active participation by all the people is the aim to be considered before all else.
>
> *Constitution on the Sacred Liturgy*, 14

The primary purpose of dismissing children for a separate Liturgy of the Word is to provide them with a focused environment where they are more likely

4

to become conscious, active listeners and responders to God's Word. The intention of the Liturgy of the Word with children is not to babysit or provide entertainment for the children. The celebration of the Liturgy of the Word with children is a liturgical experience that opens young people to hear and respond to God's Word in ways that enable them to be nurtured and challenged by its power, and to experience the grace of ongoing conversion to the vision and values of the Word of God.

When we facilitate the Liturgy of the Word with children, we are trying to:

- ◉ Help children to have an age-appropriate experience of the Liturgy of the Word

- ◉ Help children to apply the Word of God to their own experiences and actions

- ◉ Help children to become closer to God

- ◉ Help children to learn how to participate, both internally and externally, in the celebration of the Mass

ORIGINS OF THE RITUAL

Many readers may remember a time when it was common practice for a parish to hold a separate Mass for children on Sunday. Children attended Mass with their classmates while their parents attended Mass at a different time or in a different location. A deeper understanding of the Church as the Body of Christ undoubtedly paved the way for a more profound meaning of the liturgical assembly, which most likely contributed to the reasons why this practice fell out of use for the celebration of Sunday Mass.

The seeds for the development of the Liturgy of the Word with children can be found within the liturgical and catechetical movements of the early twentieth century. Notable leaders Josef Jungmann, SJ (1889–1975), and Virgil Michel, OSB (1890–1938), best known for their liturgical contributions, also influenced catechetical renewal. It is important to note that, historically, liturgy and catechesis were connected. This connection was emphasized during the six International Catechetical Study Weeks held between 1960 and 1971. These study weeks provide the historical

The liturgical and catechetical documents understand the special needs of children.

background for the modern catechetical movement that led to the development of the first international *General Catechetical Directory* (GCD, 1971) and the first American catechetical directory, *Sharing the Light of Faith: National Catechetical Directory* (SLF, 1978). Both of these documents declare catechesis as a form of ministry of the Word, which is closely linked to evangelization. They helped to restore the shattered link between liturgy and catechesis. This key theme continues with the current catechetical directories, the *General Directory for Catechesis* (GDC, 1997) and the *National Directory for Catechesis* (NDC, 2005). The relationship between liturgy and catechesis is most clearly seen in the *Rite of Christian Initiation of Adults* (RCIA, 1972, original US English text). The *General Directory for Catechesis* and the *National Directory for Catechesis* claim that the RCIA ought to be the model for all catechesis. Such a claim promotes the partnership of liturgy with catechesis.

There is no doubt that both the liturgical and catechetical developments of the past century influenced the contemporary development of the Liturgy of the Word with children. There is a strong interplay among these documents that influences the appropriate application of the celebration of a separate Liturgy of the Word with children, and the catechesis that flows both toward the celebration, and from it. The Second Vatican Council acknowledged the prophetic work of the early liturgical and catechetical movements. The *Constitution on the Sacred Liturgy*, promulgated on December 4, 1963, gave voice to a century of insight into liturgy and its deeper meaning for the life of the Church. The goal of CSL was to lead all to "full, conscious, and active participation in the liturgy" (CSL, 14). This important development allowed for appropriate adaptation in the liturgy to meet different people's needs (see CSL, 38).

Children were among the groups who benefited from appropriate adaptations. For the first time in its liturgical history, the Catholic Church made a deliberate outreach to children in many liturgical rites. The *Rite of Christian Initiation of Adults* includes a complete adaptation for children of catechetical age. The *Rite of Baptism for Children* was revised in a way that took account of the age of the infant. The *Rite of Penance* included a penitential service designed for children. *Pastoral Care of the Sick: Rites of Anointing and Viaticum* took account of the needs of sick children. The *Order of Christian Funerals* included prayers on the occasion of the death of a child, even of one who died before Baptism. And the *Directory for Masses with Children* introduced multiple adaptations for the celebration of the Eucharist and paved the way for the *Lectionary for Masses with Children*, as well as the composition of three entire Eucharistic Prayers for children.

The practice of celebrating a separate Liturgy of the Word with children was introduced by the groundbreaking document, the *Directory for Masses with*

Children (DMC), which was first put into use in 1973. The guidelines offered in this document were originally intended for the celebration of weekday Masses with children; however, the second chapter, which is called "Masses With Adults in Which Children Also Participate," refers to Sundays and feast days when children participate along with adults (see DMC, 16). At these Masses, care must be taken so that the children never feel neglected. The *Directory* tells us, "Sometimes, moreover, if the place itself and the nature of the community permit, it will be appropriate to celebrate the liturgy of the word, including a homily, with the children in a separate, but not too distant, room. Then, before the eucharistic liturgy begins, the children are led to the place where the adults have meanwhile celebrated their own liturgy of the word" (DMC, 17). The document's use of the word "sometimes" indicates that this is not intended to be the norm, but recent history shows that a separate Liturgy of the Word can be very beneficial for the children's experience of liturgy. In addition, other opportunities for the celebration of the Liturgy of the Word can also be prepared during the week for schoolchildren or for those participating in the parish catechetical program.

The *Lectionary for Masses with Children* was an innovation of the post-Conciliar Church. There are records of Lectionaries for Christian worship stretching back about 1,500 years, but not a single one was designed for children—until 1992. The *Lectionary for Masses with Children* maintained the basic structure of the standard *Lectionary for Mass*. The weekday readings were reduced to some seasonal passages, but Sundays carry versions of the full three-year cycle of readings. At times only one reading is offered before the Gospel. Entire readings that were difficult or easily misunderstood were omitted. The length of many was abbreviated. In rare instances the readings were replaced. Children were encouraged to sing the psalm.

The "Introduction" to the children's Lectionary explains when it may be used: "The scriptural readings contained in this Lectionary may be used at Sunday Masses when a large number of children are present along with adults, or when the children have a separate liturgy of the word, or for Masses at which most of the congregation consists of children (e.g., school Masses)" (LMC, 12). In 2005 the bishops of the United States approved a revised translation of the *Lectionary for Masses with Children*, but the Holy See has never confirmed it (given approval). Hence, the book approved in 1992 is still in use.

An Overview of the Liturgy of the Word with Children

When preparing a liturgy with children, it can be easy to focus on particular aspects rather than the liturgy as a whole. Before preparing a liturgy, take time to review the different parts of the ritual, their overall meaning, and particularities.

THE INTRODUCTORY RITES

The purpose of the Introductory Rites is to help the assembled people "come together as one" (GIRM, 39), preparing them for hearing God's Word and celebrating the Eucharist. This first part of the Mass includes the entrance procession accompanied by the opening song; the Sign of the Cross and the Greeting; the Penitential Act and Kyrie or the Rite for the Blessing and Sprinkling of Water (mostly during Easter Time); Gloria, and Collect. The children will come to church with their families and be seated with them in the main assembly. They remain for all of the Introductory Rites, participating as they are able with the songs and responses until they are called forward by the priest celebrant after the Collect (see LMC, 8).

Dismissal of the Children

The cue for the dismissal of the children will be the moment when the congregation sits down after the Collect. At this point, the priest celebrant should indicate that it is time for the children and their ministers to come forward. The priest hands the *Lectionary for Mass* or *Lectionary for Masses with Children* to the prayer leader. The priest might reference the ritual book and say:

> *Receive this book of readings*
> *and proclaim God's Word faithfully*
> *to the children entrusted to your care.*
> *Go in peace.*

Or the priest may note the action of dismissal:

> *My dear children,*
> *you will now go forth to hear God's Word,*
> *to praise God in song,*
> *and to reflect on the wonderful things*
> *   God has done for us.*
> *We will await your return*
> *so that together we may celebrate the Eucharist.*
> *Go in peace.*

The priest calls the children forward to be dismissed.

The priest celebrant may also say something else similar in his own words. As the children process out of the church, the assembly may sing a short refrain or acclamation which reflects the ritual action and the purpose of the separate liturgy. Your music director will have selected this piece of music already.

Processing

Once the priest celebrant has dismissed the children, the prayer leader should lead them in processing from the main sanctuary to the space where they will be celebrating the Liturgy of the Word. Because only the *Book of the Gospels* is carried in procession (see GIRM, 120D), it may be best practice for the prayer leader to hold the *Lectionary for Mass* or *Lectionary for Masses with Children* in a dignified way, but not in an elevated position, just as deacons, lectors, or readers do in the entrance procession at Mass. Process out, with the children following behind.

Centering

Upon arriving in the separate space, the prayer leader and children should take their places. The Lectionary should be placed on the ambo. Candles placed by the ambo should be lit at this time if they weren't lit before Mass began.

In the main assembly, the congregation sits after the Introductory Rites are over and they go straight into the First Reading. You may find that this is not practical in the Liturgy of the Word with children because the children may have become energized by the procession and need some help settling in.

Remind the children that they are in the presence of God. You may find that singing a hymn will help to regain the children's focus. Perhaps you can sing the hymn that your parish used as a gathering hymn for a second time. You will need to makes sure that hymnals or the words to the song are prepared in the worship space ahead of time.

THE LITURGY OF THE WORD

The Liturgy of the Word and the Liturgy of the Eucharist are the two primary parts of the Mass and are intimately connected. The Liturgy of the Word includes the readings, Homily, Profession of Faith, and the Universal Prayer (or Prayer of the Faithful). The children remain in the separate space until after the Prayer of the Faithful.

In the Liturgy of the Word, Christ himself, the Word made flesh, is present in the proclamation of Scripture (both Old and New Testaments). These ancient and holy texts are traditionally proclaimed from the ambo, the table of the Word—as the altar is the table of the Eucharist. This is where God speaks the truth of salvation to the gathered assembly.

In the standard Lectionary, there are always four readings at Sunday Mass: the First Reading, the Responsorial Psalm, the Second Reading, and the Gospel. The First Reading usually comes from the Old Testament, except during Easter Time, when it comes from the Acts of the Apostles. The Responsorial Psalm is usually sung, and usually comes from the Book of Psalms, although, sometimes, a Canticle from the Old or New Testaments is used. The Second Reading usually comes from the epistles, the letters that are found in the New Testament of the Bible. The Gospel Reading, which is preceded by the sung Gospel Acclamation (often "Alleluia"), always comes from one of the four accounts of the Gospel: Matthew, Mark, Luke, or John. Because the Liturgy of the Word is ritual, liturgical prayer, always use the Lectionary. Never use a printout of the readings, or some other source during liturgical prayer. Please see pages 28–33 for more detailed information about the Liturgy of the Word, the Lectionary, and the selection of readings.

First Reading

The First Reading should be proclaimed from the ambo either by the prayer leader or by a designated reader. The children should be seated during the First Reading. The reader should introduce the reading by saying, "A reading from the [insert the name of the book]" and conclude the reading by saying, "The word of the Lord." Lead the children in saying the response: "Thanks be to

God." It is important that you follow the words used in the main assembly, because this is how you teach the children to participate fully in the Mass as they grow older.

Responsorial Psalm

The Responsorial Psalm should be sung from the ambo. The children should remain seated during the psalm. Ideally, you will have a cantor who can lead the psalm. If this is the case, the cantor should sing the response once and then invite the children to repeat the sung response after him or her. The cantor should sing the verses, and the children should join in singing the response each time it is sung.

If you do not have a cantor to facilitate the singing of the psalm, you will want to collaborate with your parish music minister about your options. Perhaps you can just sing the response of the psalm through a few times with the children, or perhaps your music minister can recommend a seasonal psalm that you can learn and then repeat over the course of several weeks. It is important that you do everything that you can to ensure that this part of the celebration is sung.

Second Reading

The Second Reading is typically from one of the epistles, or letters found in the New Testament. The Second Reading should be proclaimed from the ambo, either by the prayer leader or by a designated reader. If there is no Second Reading, either because you chose to omit a reading or because you are using the *Lectionary for Masses with Children* and no Second Reading is listed, then you should proceed straight from the psalm to the Gospel Acclamation.

The children should remain seated for the Second Reading. The reader should conclude by saying, "The word of the Lord." Lead the children in responding, "Thanks be to God."

Gospel Acclamation

The Gospel Acclamation, typically "Alleluia," except during Lent, is sung prior to the reading of the Gospel. The "Introduction" to the *Lectionary for Masses with Children* notes that "the gospel acclamation must always be sung" (LMC, 51). Your parish music director can introduce you to a simple Alleluia refrain (or alternate Lenten acclamation) that can be taught to the children once and used repeatedly over the course of a season. The prayer leader or cantor can sing the refrain once, and the children can sing it back. The children should stand at the start of the Gospel Acclamation.

Gospel Reading

Children should stand for the Gospel.

The children should remain standing for the Gospel Reading. The Gospel should be read by the prayer leader or by another designated reader. Only an ordained minister uses the greeting, "The Lord be with you." More often than not, a layperson will proclaim the Gospel. The lay reader should omit the greeting and begin by saying, "A reading from the holy Gospel according to . . ." and should name the source of the Gospel (for example, "A reading from the holy Gospel according to Matthew"). Lead the children in responding, "Glory to you, O Lord," while signing themselves with the cross on their foreheads, lips, and hearts. At the conclusion of the Gospel Reading, the reader should say, "The Gospel of the Lord." Lead the children in responding, "Praise to you, Lord Jesus Christ." After this, they may be seated.

Homily or Explanation of the Scripture Readings

The children should be seated for the Homily or explanation of the Scripture readings (or reflection). The Homily or reflection should be led by the priest, deacon, or prayer leader. It can be led from the ambo, or if the leader finds it more comfortable to lead from another place, that is fine, too. The Homily or reflection is important because it explains the readings and allows the children to explore the meaning of the text in their own lives. The Homily or reflection in Masses with children may take a somewhat different form than it usually does in the main assembly. Rather than simply speaking to the children, it is effective to allow the Homily or reflection to take the form of a dialogue with the children (see DMC, 48). Please see pages 34–37 for more information about the nature of the Homily and reflection and how to prepare effectively.

The Creed or Profession of Faith

Following the Homily or reflection, you should lead the children in the Profession of Faith, or Creed. You may say the Nicene Creed, which is typically used at Mass, or the Apostles' Creed, which is a somewhat shorter version of the Creed and is often used with children. If the children have already learned or will soon be learning the Apostles' Creed by heart, you may find it more appropriate to use that version. The children should stand for the Profession of Faith. Lead the children in bowing at the appropriate point in the prayer. During the Nicene Creed, you should bow during the words, "and by the Holy Spirit was incarnate of the Virgin Mary, / and became man." During the Apostles' Creed, you should bow during the words, "who was conceived by the Holy Spirit, born of the Virgin Mary." If the children do not yet know these prayers by heart and are likely to struggle to get through them, you may want to display the words on a poster or projector, or speak one line of the prayer at a time, having the children repeat each line after you.

The Universal Prayer or Prayer of the Faithful

The Universal Prayer (or Prayer of the Faithful) is our time as a gathered community to respond to the Word of God and pray for the needs and salvation of the world. The children should remain standing during the Prayer of the Faithful. The petitions can be read by the prayer leader or another designated reader. Lead the children in saying the response to each petition. You may want to invite the children to add petitions of their own after the written petitions have all been read. Respond to the children's petitions with the response. You may use the petitions composed for the main assembly or you may compose them yourself. You will want to put the intentions in a binder appropriate to be used during the liturgy. Consult with your liturgy director about what to use. Pages 38–41 in this resource provides additional information for writing the petitions.

Closing Song

You may choose to conclude with another short song, especially if the children have become enthusiastic in suggesting their own petitions. They may need to be calmed a bit before returning to the main assembly. Remember to consult with your music director about music options.

Returning to the Main Assembly

The children should return to the main assembly by the start of the Liturgy of the Eucharist, after the main assembly has finished the Prayer of the Faithful. An assistant can help ensure that you return at the right time by checking on the progress of the main assembly and alerting you when they have begun the Creed. Process back to the main assembly with the children and tell them that they should quietly return to their places in the pews. Keep an eye out for any children who are having difficulty finding their families. This concludes the

Liturgy of the Word. From this point, the children will celebrate the Liturgy of the Eucharist and Concluding Rites along with the rest of the main assembly.

Silence

Before concluding this section, something must be said about the use of silence throughout the Liturgy of the Word. The *Directory for Masses with Children* makes special mention of the importance of silence: "Even in Masses with children 'silence should be observed at the designated times as part of the celebration' lest too great a place be given to external action. In their own way, children are genuinely capable of reflection" (DMC, 37). The *General Instruction of the Roman Missal* is the document which provides the directions for how to celebrate the Mass. This document specifies that silence should be incorporated into the liturgy at these specific places during the Liturgy of the Word: after the readings or after the Homily (see GIRM, 45). Moments of silence in the liturgy give us space to meditate on what we have experienced or to praise God and pray to him in our hearts. When you teach children how to feel comfortable in silence between readings and after the Homily or reflection, you are teaching them the ritual language of the Church. There is so much noise in our world, and a little silence can do us a lot of good. Of course, the children should also be silent when returning to the main assembly.

Preparing for the Liturgy of the Word with Children

A PERSON OF PRAYER

As you work to establish good practices for the celebration of the Liturgy of the Word with children within your parish, it can be easy to obsess about the details or "rules." As a result, you might forget that a truly effective prayer leader is a

Leaders of children's Liturgy of the Word should be persons of prayer.

person of deep faith and personal spirituality. Children are easily engaged in a spirit of worship. If the leader is a genuine person of faith and prayer who loves children, they will respond readily and wholeheartedly in a spirit of worship. If not, the children will sense when the order and details of the Liturgy of the Word overtake the proclamation of the Good News and praise of God as most important, and they will begin to point out "mistakes" in the celebration. Children intuitively know and respond to faithful, prayerful leaders.

Prepare to celebrate the Liturgy of the Word with children by engaging yourself in regular prayer. During the week, take time in prayer with the Scripture readings that you will be proclaiming on Sunday. Be mindful of the themes in the readings as you go through your daily life, keeping your eyes open for ways in which they are illuminated or illustrated by your experiences and encounters. This will make your own experience of your ministry more meaningful, and will also make you a better prayer leader as you celebrate the Word with children. As the "Introduction" to the *Lectionary for Masses with Children* notes, "Children imitate the behaviors and attitudes of adults. For this reason, adults who serve as ministers at liturgical celebrations where children are present should conduct the entire range of liturgical actions, gestures, and songs with dignity and care" (LMC, 23).

There are many resources on the market that provide prayers and spiritual reflections related to the Sunday readings. You might consider investing in one of these products to guide you in your prayer life. You can also find ample material of this nature on the Internet.

Before you begin the Liturgy of the Word, take time to offer yourself to God as an instrument that he will use to facilitate the growth of the children's relationship with him. Even if you only have a few minutes (or seconds!) to spare before beginning the Liturgy of the Word, use that time to take a deep breath, center yourself in God's presence, and offer yourself and your ministry over to him.

REVIEW THE SCRIPTURE READINGS

Prior to each celebration of the Liturgy of the Word with children, prayer leaders should review the Scripture readings for the day, using the version of the Lectionary that you will be using when you lead the Liturgy of the Word (either the standard Lectionary or the *Lectionary for Masses with Children*). It is also particularly helpful to read through the cycle of readings for an entire season, especially Advent, Christmas Time, Lent, and Easter Time. This broad overview will put your ministry not only in the context of a particular Sunday, but also in the entire seasonal movement. You will want to refer to pages 28–33 in this resource to familiarize yourself with the two options for Lectionary texts, how to use the Lectionary, and how to adapt the readings, if necessary.

Knowing the readings ahead of time helps the leader to focus on a particular message and strategize how to approach it with the children. Familiarity with the text also encourages the leader to discover the meanings of any unfamiliar words, or the identities of unfamiliar people long before he or she is in the room with the children. You may find that a study edition of a Catholic Bible will assist you in your preparation (although it is best not to use the Bible during liturgy).

As a prayer leader, it is your job to make the words of the Homily or reflection your own. You will want to rehearse your Homily or reflection ahead of time so that you can engage the children better. Another characteristic of good homiletics is the ability to understand the assembly and relate your words to their lived experience. When you do this with children, you help them to bring what they hear at church into their daily lives. A good Homily or reflection will inspire the children to respond with sentiments of praise, joy, hope, and gratitude.

LITURGICAL MUSIC

Music plays an important role in good liturgical celebrations. There are several sung parts of the Liturgy of the Word, including the Responsorial Psalm (sung between the First Reading and the Second Reading on Sundays) and the Gospel Acclamation (the Alleluia [or alternate Lenten acclamation] sung before the reading from the Gospel). The "Introduction" to the *Lectionary for Masses with Children* clearly calls for these elements to be sung: "liturgy requires the full use of music which is integral to the whole celebration, including the proclamation of the word of God. The responsorial psalm is normally sung by a cantor with the assembly singing the refrain. The gospel acclamation must always be sung" (LMC, 51).

Music is therefore a sign of God's love for us and of our love for him. . . .
Music make[s] the liturgical prayers of the Christian community
more alive and fervent so that everyone can praise and beseech the
Triune God more powerfully, more intently and more effectively.
Sing the Lord: Music in Divine Worship,
2, 5; quoting MSD, no. 31; see no. 33

Many adult leaders of the Liturgy of the Word with children find music to be an especially challenging component of the celebration of the Word. Those who are not musically trained can feel insecure when selecting or leading music. When selecting music, you will want to involve your parish music minister. You should consider the music that will be sung in the main assembly and see how you can best make it accessible and engaging for the children. It is best if the music used in your celebration of the Word mirrors the music that is used in the main assembly. This gives children the chance to learn the songs that the rest of the parish community is singing and prepares them for fuller participation in the Mass. In most cases, the music will already be selected for you. The music director will have selected the song which accompanies the dismissal of the children to a separate place of prayer. The music director will already have selected the setting of the Responsorial Psalm and the Gospel Acclamation for the main assembly. Any additional pieces of music are added elements. In these cases, it is the responsibility of the prayer leader.

Singing must be given great importance in all celebrations, but it is to be especially encouraged in every way for Masses celebrated with children, in view of their special affinity for music.

Directory for Masses with Children, 30

Because the Liturgy of the Word with children is *liturgical* prayer, then the music you select should be *liturgical* music. The parish hymnal is the best place to start. The music should reflect the liturgical season and the texts of the song should connect to or highlight aspects of the Scripture readings. Simple texts and songs with refrains work best with children. It is always best to talk with your music director about options. They will have many suggestions of songs to use.

Live music led by trained music ministers is ideal. Consult your parish music minister to see if there may be a musician who is available to lead song with the children. Sometimes a teen or one of the children's parents might be willing to

serve in this role. If there is no option for live accompaniment or a trained cantor, your leaders will have to do their best to facilitate joyful song on their own. You may want to have simple musical instruments such as chimes or bells that the children can play as they sing. If you fear that the children are too young to learn whole songs, your leaders can sing with them by using the "call and response" method, singing one line to them and inviting them to sing it back to the leader. Your parish music ministry staff will be able to help you with any questions you might have.

Live music is always preferred.

THE UNIVERSAL PRAYER OR PRAYER OF THE FAITHFUL

As mentioned before, you will need to prepare the Prayer of the Faithful in a way that is appropriate for children. The texts used in the main assembly may be adapted or you may write your own. The Church has specific criteria for composing these prayers. Please refer to pages 38–41 for guidance.

THE LITURGICAL ENVIRONMENT

In order to help the children carry the deep reverence that they feel for the sacred space of the church into their space for the Liturgy of the Word, careful attention must be given to liturgical environment. The space should be arranged and decorated as a liturgical space, not a classroom or play space. When preparing the liturgical environment of the space for prayer, keep in mind that it should facilitate the "full, conscious, and active participation" (CSL, 14) of the gathered assembly. Environment speaks of the sacred and aids in the communication of reverence, wonder, and awe.

When preparing the separate space for the Liturgy of the Word with children, as much as possible, attention needs to be given to beauty, color, seating, and furnishing. The character of this space must reflect the main worship space and allow for procession, song, appropriate movement, and prayer. The ambo, or table of the Word, is of great importance here. The presence of a proper ambo teaches the children reverence for the Word. A candle of sufficient size for the space will demonstrate that Christ, the Light of *The presence of the ambo reflects the* the World, is with us in the proclamation of the *importance of and reverence given* Word. The presence of a crucifix stands as a pal- *to the Word of God.* pable sign that, in and through the Liturgy of the Word, we are still immersed in the Paschal Mystery. In general, the choice of decoration ought to reflect the style of the main worship space. For example, a simple drape for the color of the season should be visible. If flowers adorn the sanctuary in the main worship space, flowers can also beautify the separate worship space. In other words, keep it simple and meaningful. It is very effective when the liturgy committee or liturgical environment committee that oversees and prepares the main worship space collaborates with the preparers of the Liturgy of the Word with children, because the goal of liturgy with children is full participation with the adult assembly. The *Directory for Masses with Children* encourages the use of children's artwork to be displayed. The art can be an illustrations "of a homily, as visual expressions of the intentions of the [Universal Prayer], or as inspirations to reflection" (DMC, 36). It is important to note that these illustrations and artwork should not be a project to be done during the Liturgy of the Word. A prayer leader and the parish liturgist might collaborate with religious education teachers to connect what they celebrate during the liturgy with their religious formation classes.

If you are using a classroom, rearrange the chairs and move desks out of the way. Remember to consider the space in relation to the movement associated with the celebration so that you and the children can participate in the procession and the proclamation of the Word with ease and grace. Put away any toys or games, and do your best to temporarily remove or cover any distracting posters or displays. Create a space where the Lectionary, candle, and any other liturgical symbols are prominent and easily seen.

The liturgy of the Mass contains many visual elements and these should be given great prominence with children. . . . In addition to the visual elements that belong to the celebration and to the place of celebration, it is appropriate to introduce other elements that will permit children to perceive visually the wonderful works of God in creation and redemption and thus support their prayer. The liturgy should never appear as something dry and merely intellectual.

Directory for Masses with Children, 35

The individual leader's involvement in preparing the space for Liturgy of the Word with children will vary from parish to parish. Some leaders may have little input into the setup of the space, while others may be asked to arrange the room. In general, the area in which the children will encounter the Word of God should encourage reverence. Many parishes have a liturgical environment team or other volunteers that might be willing to help you, or that might have great ideas for blending the children's environment with the main worship space.

OTHER LITURGICAL MINISTERS

It may seem easier to just perform all of the ministries of the Liturgy of the Word yourself, rather than try to involve other ministers. The *Directory for Masses with Children*, however, clearly calls for the use of ministers, when possible: "Even in Masses with children attention is to be paid to the diversity of ministries so that the Mass may stand out clearly as the celebration of a community. For example, readers and cantors, whether children or adults, should be employed. In this way a variety of voices will keep the children from becoming bored" (DMC, 24).

Some of the ministers you should consider involving in your celebration include:

READERS: These are the people who proclaim the Scripture readings. You might use a different reader for each of the Scripture readings, as we often do in the main assembly, or if that is not practical, you might use the same reader for each of the readings. Children may proclaim the readings, but keep in mind that preparation is a key part of this ministry. Typically, the children who come to the Liturgy of the Word with children have not received training as readers, and do not have time to prepare the readings well ahead of time. It is better to have the readings proclaimed by adults who have had time to prepare than by untrained and unprepared children.

MUSIC MINISTERS: It is ideal for music to be led by a cantor, with live accompaniment. Talk to your parish music minister to see what can be arranged. Perhaps one or two of the choir members can be spared to come down to sing with the children during the Liturgy of the Word. If it is not possible for your parish music minister to arrange anything, consider what other options might exist for you. Perhaps there is a parent of one of the children or a teen in the parish who can perform this role.

READERS OF THE PRAYER OF THE FAITHFUL: In the main assembly, the intercessions for the Prayer of the Faithful (the Universal Prayer) are read by the deacon or by a lay minister. One of the adults or teens who is helping to lead the Liturgy of the Word with children may be selected for this role. If you must use children as readers in your celebration of the Word, perhaps using them as readers during the Prayer of the Faithful will be more suitable than having them proclaim the Scripture.

INVOLVING ASSISTANTS

You will want to have a number of assistants appropriate to the number of children in your group (at least one per every ten children) in order to help you maintain a prayerful atmosphere. Assistants can help you process with the children to and from the main assembly and can watch out for any children who are acting out or having trouble sitting still in order to quietly help them. You will want to assign an assistant or two to care for any children who need to use the restroom or who do not want to remain apart from their families and need to return to the main assembly before the conclusion of the Liturgy of the Word. You will also want to assign an assistant to watch the progress of the Liturgy of the Word in the main assembly to be sure that you return at the appropriate time.

Everyone who participates in the Liturgy of the Word with children need to have some basic training in and awareness of their liturgical role. The same care should be given to their preparation as is given to those who serve as liturgical ministers in the main assembly. It is important for those who serve as liturgical ministers in the celebration of the Word with children to be aware of and comfortable with the fact that they are involved in a full liturgical experience, not instruction, a time for play, or a child-care experience.

When recruiting assistants, music ministers, or other adults to participate in any aspect of the Liturgy of the Word with children, be sure to check with your parish or diocese to find out about the conditions under which they may work with children. It may be necessary for them to undergo training or background screening (see page 46). As an adult who has been given the tremendous honor of caring for the spiritual development of children, it is your responsibility to ensure that they can develop their relationship with God in a safe and nurturing environment.

USE OF CRAFTS

In many places, children's Liturgy of the Word involves worksheets and craft projects. Many of the resources available for children's Liturgy of the Word make explicit use of activity pages and so on. It is important to note, though, that the *Directory for Masses with Children* and the "Introduction" to the *Lectionary for Masses with Children* never recommend crafts or activities. It is recommended that you use crafts very sparingly, if at all, and that you avoid any type of worksheet or activity page that will seem reminiscent of schoolwork or Vacation Bible School activities. For most readings, crafts are unnecessary, and just serve as busywork rather than as aids to reflection. For example, in the story about Peter denying Jesus, there would be nothing to be gained from having the children color in pictures of Jesus and Peter. It is a powerful story of love and forgiveness to which the children can easily relate without needing to create any kind of visual aid.

On very rare occasions, a simple coloring activity may be a fruitful aid in reflection. For example, if talking about the reading for the Second Sunday of Advent, Year A (Isaiah 11:1–10; *Lectionary for Mass*, #4), you might focus on the line "the wolf shall be a guest of the lamb," by engaging in a discussion of the two animals while the children draw pictures of them together. The discussion might focus on why the two animals don't share the same living space here on earth, and what Isaiah might be telling us about the kingdom of God by saying that the one will be the guest of the other. This craft is not busywork, but is a means of delving deeper into reflection on the passage. This type of approach lends itself well to pulling the children deeper into passages that contain vibrant but abstract imagery. If you are going to reflect on Scripture by drawing, it is best to have the children do it in a simple way by handing out sheets of paper and crayons. More involved craft projects that involve scissors, glue, multiple steps, and so on, are not appropriate for the celebration of the Liturgy of the Word.

The children should not return to the main assembly carrying sheets of paper or craft projects. These can become a distraction in the pew, and contribute to the children's feeling that the Liturgy of the Word is a "break" from Mass. If you absolutely must send sheets of paper or activity pages home with the children, see if you can arrange a method for the parents and children to come collect their work after the Mass has ended. Perhaps the leader of children's Liturgy of the Word can stand to one side of the doorway next to the person distributing bulletins, and can distribute materials to families as they exit. You may not want to send drawings home at all, and instead consider alternate options that will help the children to understand that any drawing they do during the Liturgy of the Word has a different focus to it than a drawing they do at school or art class. For example, if you were to have them draw pictures of the wolf being the guest of the lamb (as in the example above), perhaps you might collect these images and use them as part of your liturgical environment for the remainder of Advent, inviting the children to use the artwork as a means of ongoing reflection. The image of the wolf being the guest of the lamb might be interesting to discuss again, for example, on the following Sunday when we hear from Isaiah 35:1-6a, 10 about how the wilderness and the parched land will rejoice and bloom with flowers.

REVIEWING RESOURCES

In order to write a good reflection for the children and lead prayer effectively, you will want to consult additional Scripture resources and needed liturgical resources. Some resources provide an entire session outline or script to use (such as *Children's Liturgy of the Word: A Weekly Resource* published by Liturgy Training Publications). Always review the outlines and scripts ahead of time. Please see pages 53–56 for suggestions for resources.

WORSHIP AIDS FOR CHILDREN

Worship aids—printed programs containing hymns and spoken or sung responses—are very helpful in encouraging the "full, conscious, and active participation" (CSL, 14) of adults in the liturgy. What about children? Should we prepare a worship aid for them?

The answer to this question will definitely vary. In general, a worship aid would seem unnecessary for the short time the children are gathering for the Liturgy of the Word. But if you wish to focus in on some of the texts of the liturgy—for example, the Creed—having the text printed can be helpful to invite discussion of a particular text. If you are introducing a new song, printing the text with the music can be helpful as well. Whatever you decide, keep in mind that the worship aid, to be useful, needs to be clear, legible, and necessary. If a worship aid is handed out and not used regularly throughout the prayer, it will simply be a distracting piece of paper. Make sure that whatever you hand out is used throughout. You might find it more helpful to write the refrain to the Responsorial Psalm and the text of the Creed on a large board. And given that our goal in the liturgy for adults is to hear the readings, not read them for ourselves, it seems advisable to start young by encouraging children to read the readings in advance of the liturgy—not during it.

LOGISTICS

Make sure you are aware of physical logistics and choreography for the Liturgy of the Word. You should know where your parish keeps the *Lectionary for Masses with Children* or the standard Lectionary that will be used for the Liturgy of the Word with children, and who prepares the ritual book before the liturgy begins. You will want to know how and where to gather the children after the Collect, how to process from the main sanctuary with the children, where to lead the children, and how the children are to sit once they arrive. You will need to know all of the logistics of the space where you will lead the Liturgy of the Word with children, including how to turn on the lights, who to contact if the door is locked, and where the ambo and other liturgical environment pieces are located if they are not permanent. You should be shown restrooms that the children may use. You should know how to process with the children back to the main sanctuary, and should have a strategy for helping any children who are having difficulty finding their parents in the pews. Consult with your parish staff if you are unsure.

The Liturgical Year

The liturgical year is the Church's way of telling the Christian story daily, weekly, and yearly. The liturgical year is not a reenactment of the life of Jesus. Rather, it gives meaning to past, unrepeatable events so that the Church can remember and celebrate the presence of Jesus Christ, crucified, risen, and among us today. The liturgical year consists of the six seasons and individual celebrations for the saints. When celebrating the Liturgy of the Word with children on Sundays, prayer leaders need only be concerned with the seasonal cycle. Being familiar with the liturgical year is important, for it helps us know what readings to use, and it shapes our understanding of these seasonal readings, as well as guiding the selection of music and the seasonal environment. Children may also have questions about the liturgical year and the change in colors.

SUNDAY: THE DAY THE LORD HAS MADE

For Christians, Sunday was the original feast of the liturgical year. Dating back to the time of the Apostles, Sunday was the day for celebrating the Paschal Mystery. It was the day to gather the community to hear the Word and break bread in Eucharist. The Second Vatican Council, and the liturgical movement that preceded it, restored Sunday to its original meaning. In our Church today, the Sunday gathering of the people of God is a brilliant sign of God's saving work in and through Jesus Christ. The celebration of the Liturgy of the Word with children is an opportunity to demonstrate the uniqueness of Sunday, especially in a time when, for many families, other activities often take precedence over celebrating the Eucharist.

ADVENT AND CHRISTMAS TIME

Advent begins with Evening Prayer I of the Sunday closest to November 30, and ends before Evening Prayer I on the Solemnity of the Nativity of the Lord (Christmas), and the liturgical color is violet. The season of Advent is twofold in character. It is a time of preparation for Christmas when we remember the first coming of Christ, and it also draws our attention toward Christ's second coming at the end of time. The Lectionary readings for this time offer rich images of waiting and preparation, and introduce us to key figures including the prophet Isaiah, John the Baptist, and Mary, the Holy Mother of God.

Christmas Time celebrates the Nativity of the Lord. The season goes from Evening Prayer I of the Solemnity of the Nativity of the Lord (Christmas) up to Evening Prayer II on the Sunday after the Solemnity of the Epiphany of the Lord (usually the Feast of the Baptism of the Lord), and the liturgical colors are white and gold. Christmas Time presents two challenges for those who work with children. The first is helping children and their families to understand that the celebration of Christmas Time has only begun on Christmas Day, and that it lasts for several days beyond that. The other challenge is that children often view Christmas historically, seeing it as a celebration of Jesus being born long ago, and not as a celebration of God with us now. In your time with the children, you will want to be careful not to cater to their historical perception by doing things like discussing Christmas as a celebration of Jesus's birthday or by only focusing on the events of Jesus's birth in his time, and not of Jesus's ongoing presence and the meaning of the Incarnation in our lives today. You will also want to avoid the tradition of the Christmas pageant. Christmas pageants have their place, but they should never take place during Mass and do not belong in the Liturgy of the Word with children. The "Introduction" to the *Lectionary for Masses with Children* makes it clear that pageants have no place in the Liturgy of the Word: "The Mass is not an historical reenactment of the events of salvation history and care should be taken not to give the impression that the liturgy of the word is a play" (LMC, 52). Preparers of the Liturgy of the Word with children have an opportunity to stress the fact that during Christmas Time we celebrate God with us now.

LENT, SACRED PASCHAL TRIDUUM, AND EASTER TIME

Lent begin with Ash Wednesday and continues up until the celebration of the Mass of the Lord's Supper on Holy Thursday evening. Lent prepares us to celebrate the Paschal Mystery in a unique way. As catechumens prepare for Baptism at the Easter Vigil, the baptized prepare to renew their baptismal promises. This preparation is very important to the character of Lent. It gives deeper meaning to the traditional practices of prayer, fasting, and almsgiving. The liturgical color for Lent is violet.

The Sacred Paschal Triduum begins with the celebration of the Mass of the Lord's Supper on Holy Thursday evening and ends with Evening Prayer on Easter Sunday. The Paschal Triduum is the highest holy time of the liturgical year. It maintains the original, ancient aspect of Easter: Death and Resurrection. The Triduum presents tradition at its best, and children can benefit greatly from the richness of the liturgies celebrated on Holy Thursday, Good Friday, and Holy Saturday. It is imperative to understand that the Paschal Triduum is not three separate liturgical celebrations. It is one liturgy that is so rich that it takes three days to celebrate it.

The Sacred Paschal Triduum is followed by the fifty-day celebration of Easter Time. The liturgical colors for Easter Time are white and gold. You will want to help the children with whom you work with to understand that Easter is more than one day. It is a season that is celebrated from Easter Sunday through Pentecost Sunday. This is the time to revel in the Resurrection and mediate upon hope fulfilled. The readings proclaimed during this season communicate the wonder of who we are as the baptized. Here and now, we are renewed for mission. We are reminded of new life and Baptism by the sprinkling rite celebrated on Sundays during Easter Time and by the colors and symbols of the Easter environment.

ORDINARY TIME

There is nothing ordinary about Ordinary Time. This period of thirty-three or thirty-four weeks celebrates the mystery of Christ outside of the highpoints of the Lent/Triduum/Easter Time and Advent/Christmas Time cycles. During Ordinary Time, we learn that we meet the risen Lord in the seemingly ordinary, everyday aspects of our lives. Ordinary Time begins after Evening Prayer II on the Sunday after the Solemnity of the Epiphany of the Lord, and continues through the Tuesday before Ash Wednesday. It begins again after Evening Prayer II on the Solemnity of Pentecost and ends before Evening Prayer I on the First Sunday of Advent. The liturgical color for Ordinary Time is green.

The Scripture Readings

THE *LECTIONARY FOR MASS* AND *LECTIONARY FOR MASSES WITH CHILDREN*

The Scripture that is used in the Liturgy of the Word with children on Sunday should come from either the standard *Lectionary for Mass* or the *Lectionary for Masses with Children,* using the readings that are proper for that day. You will need to consult with your pastor or liturgist as to which Lectionary readings will be proclaimed during the celebration of the Liturgy of the Word with children. Both Lectionaries include an "Introduction" which is very important for all prayer leaders to read. These introductions provide theological reflection on the importance of the Scriptures proclaimed at liturgy and guidance for how to celebrate the Liturgy of the Word properly.

The standard *Lectionary for Mass* is the ritual book that includes all of the readings that will be used in the main assembly in your parish. The standard *Lectionary for Mass* is usually four volumes. The first volume is the one you use the most because it contains the readings for Sunday. The second and third volumes are used for weekdays, and the fourth includes the readings for other special occasions. This Lectionary always has to be used at Masses attended by the main assembly. In addition to the four volumes, some parishes may have additional volumes for the Sunday Lectionary—one volume for each cycle of readings.

The Church's pastoral care for children prompted the approval of the *Lectionary for Masses with Children* for use in the dioceses of the United States in 1994. It is intended for use at Masses with children, and not for regular Sunday Masses (that is, a Mass with the main assembly, see LMC, 13). The *Lectionary for Masses with Children* adheres to the principle of adaptation reflected in the *Directory for Masses with Children* so that children may be nourished in faith and led to full, active, and conscious participation with the assembly (see DMC, 22). This Lectionary includes readings that have been adapted for use with children. The translation of the Scripture has been simplified so that children can better understand the readings they hear at Mass.

> The scriptural readings contained in [the *Lectionary for Masses with Children*] may be used at Sunday Masses when a large number of children are present along with adults, or when the children have a separate liturgy of the word, or for Masses at which most of the congregation consists of children (e.g., school Masses). . . .
>
> Proper balance and consideration for the entire assembly should be observed. Therefore, priest celebrants should not use this *Lectionary for Masses with Children* exclusively or even preferentially at Sunday Masses even though large numbers of children are present.
>
> "Introduction," *Lectionary for Masses with Children*, 12, 13

FINDING AND SELECTING THE READINGS IN THE LECTIONARY

To locate the readings for Sunday Mass in the Lectionary, you need to know whether you are in Year A, Year B, or Year C. The Sunday *Lectionary for Mass* and the *Lectionary for Masses with Children* both follow a three-year cycle of readings for Sunday. Notice the letter on the spine of your Lectionary—A, B, or C. Years A, B, and C are the designations of each Lectionary cycle, each year features one Gospel: Matthew for Year A, Mark for Year B, and Luke for Year C. If you're confused as to what year you are in, always consult with your pastor or liturgist. However, here is a helpful tip: If the four-digit number of the calendar year is divisible exactly by three, then we are in Year C. You can figure out Year A and B from there. The liturgical year begins, of course, with the Advent that precedes the new calendar year.

Once you know which year of the Lectionary you are in, it is easy to find the readings. You'll notice that every Sunday is assigned a distinctive number. This is very helpful as these numbers are unique to each set of readings. If the Sunday readings for today are to be found at #60B, you'll find only one set of readings with that number no matter how many volumes of the Lectionary you thumb through—#60B refers to the readings for the Seventh Sunday of Easter in Year B in the standard Lectionary.

If you don't know what the distinctive number is, you can also find your readings by the name of the Sunday. As you page through the Lectionary, you will notice that the book is arranged by seasons: Advent, Christmas Time, Lent, Easter Time, and Ordinary Time. Following the readings for Ordinary Time is a special section for Solemnities and Feasts of the Lord during Ordinary Time, where you will find the readings for days like the Most Holy Trinity and the Most Holy Body and Blood of Christ. So, for example, if this coming Sunday is the Second Sunday in Advent you will first want to locate the section for Advent. Within that seasonal section, the Sundays are ordered sequentially by the number of the Sunday. Simply find the Second Sunday in Advent, and you're all set.

Your parish liturgist or pastor should let you know ahead of time the name of the Sunday or the proper Lectionary number. This information is also in your parish's seasonal missal or music supplement. *The Daily Mass Readings: A Simple Reference Guide* is a great resource for knowing what readings to use. Published annually by Liturgy Training Publications, this resource includes the Lectionary numbers for the regular Lectionary for each day of the liturgical year. Simply find the date and you know what readings to use!

You should be aware that the numbers for a given Sunday are different in the *Lectionary for Mass* and the *Lectionary for Masses with Children*. For example, in the regular Lectionary, the number for the First Sunday of Lent, Year B, is 23. In the children's Lectionary it is 19. It can be confusing. You should always check with your pastor or liturgist to know a) what Lectionary to use and b) what the Lectionary number is for the particular Sunday (for example, First Sunday of Lent).

THE STRUCTURE OF THE LITURGY OF THE WORD

The Lectionary includes four readings for every Sunday: the First Reading (usually from the Old Testament except during Easter when it is from Acts of the Apostles), the Responsorial Psalm, the Second Reading (usually from one of the epistles), and the Gospel. The First Reading usually comes from somewhere in the Old Testament. It always bears a thematic relationship to the Gospel. During other times of the year, the First Reading explores a theme relating to the season. For example, the First Readings of Lent tell a sequence of stories from salvation history leading up to the promise of our redemption. Over the course of three years, nearly all of the books of the Old Testament are represented in the Sunday Lectionary.

An exception to this plan occurs during Easter Time. At that time, the First Reading is drawn from the New Testament—from the Acts of the Apostles. There we hear the story of the apostolic Church as it faced struggles and rejoiced in the promise of the Resurrection. For the seven weeks of Easter, all the readings come from the New Testament.

The Responsorial Psalm relates to a theme from the First Reading. There are a few exceptions when the psalm pertains more to the season of the year or even to the Gospel. It is permissible to substitute another psalm that fits the occasion, especially if the parish has a musical setting of it in its repertoire. Seasonal options are provided in the Lectionary. When leading the music at a separate Liturgy of the Word with children, it is best to use the same setting of the psalm that is sung by the main assembly.

The readings come from either the standard Lectionary or the Lectionary for Masses with Children.

The Second Readings during Ordinary Time are semi-continuous excerpts of different New Testament books. For example, each year Ordinary Time begins with a series of readings from Paul's first letter to the Corinthians. Large parts of the letter are never read, but the passages we hear follow the thought of the letter from beginning to end over the entire three-year cycle. During the other times of the year, the Second Reading is chosen because it relates to the feast or season being celebrated. For example, the Second Readings of Advent show how the early Christians expected Christ would come again very soon, and how they challenged one another to live accordingly.

ADAPTING THE READINGS FOR CHILDREN

The *Directory for Masses with Children* states that, with the consent of the pastor, it is permissible for leaders of prayer to choose to shorten or omit some readings so long as the Gospel is always proclaimed. So, if you are using the standard Lectionary, you will want to review the readings prior to each Mass in order to determine what adaptations you might need to make in accordance with the wishes of your pastor. It is permissible to work with your pastor or his designated delegate to omit or truncate readings, so long as the Gospel reading is always proclaimed. When deciding which readings to do, quality, rather than quantity, should always be your measure. "Everything depends on the spiritual advantage that the reading can bring to the children" (DMC, 44). A shorter reading may not necessarily be more appropriate for the children than a longer one. If you do elect to omit or truncate readings, it should be done so as to aid the children's understanding. If you do choose to truncate a reading, you will want to do so carefully and in consultation with your pastor or liturgist. The *Directory for Masses with Children* says that truncating readings should be done in a way that "the meaning of the text or the intent and, as it were, style of the Scriptures are not distorted" (DMC, 43).

With regard to the number of readings on Sundays and holy days, the decrees of the conferences of bishops are to be observed. If three or even two readings appointed on Sundays or weekdays can be understood by the children only with difficulty, it is permissible to read two or only one of them, but the reading of the gospel should never be omitted.

Directory for Masses with Children, 42

If you are using the *Lectionary for Masses with Children,* then the work of adaptation has already been done for you. You will find that the readings have already been omitted, shortened, and replaced as deemed necessary by the creators of the *Lectionary for Masses with Children.* There are a few instances where the preparers of the *Lectionary for Masses with Children* thought that one reading would be too difficult for children and that another reading might do better in its place. So, you will find some cases where the First Reading or the Second Reading in the *Lectionary for Masses with Children* is an entirely different reading than the one found in the standard Lectionary that the main assembly will be hearing and listening to at Sunday Mass. You will want to take note of the infrequent instances where one of the readings in the *Lectionary for Masses with Children* may be different from the reading that will be heard in the main assembly. Parents should be made aware when the readings are different so that they are not confused if they try to discuss the readings with their children.

If you are using the standard Lectionary and preparing to use all of the readings, then this organization is clear. But if you plan to omit one reading, it can become confusing. If, for example, you omit the First Reading, does that mean that you start with the Responsorial Psalm? The *Lectionary for Masses with Children* provides some guidance on this point. When the First Reading is omitted in the *Lectionary for Masses with Children,* the Second Reading moves forward to take its place. Take this example from the Twelfth Sunday in Ordinary Time, Year C:

	Lectionary for Mass (#96)	Lectionary for Masses with Children (#91)
FIRST READING	Zechariah 12:10–11; 13:1	Galatians 3:26–29
RESPONSORIAL PSALM	Psalm 63:2, 3–4, 5-6, 8-9	Psalm 100:1–2, 3, 5
SECOND READING	Galatians 3:26–29	No Second Reading
GOSPEL ACCLAMATION	John 10:27	John 10:27
GOSPEL READING	Luke 9:18–24	Luke 9:18–24

As you can see, the *Lectionary for Masses with Children* omits the reading from Zechariah and bumps up what was the Second Reading in the standard Lectionary, the reading from Galatians, to take its place. The Responsorial Psalm is sung after the Galatians reading, and is followed directly by the Gospel Acclamation and Gospel. When the Second Reading from the standard Lectionary is omitted in the *Lectionary for Masses with Children*, then essentially the same thing happens: the Responsorial Psalm is followed directly by the Gospel Acclamation and Gospel.

Preparing the Homily or Explanation of the Scripture Readings

The Homily is a specific kind of preaching. While a sermon may take a wide variety of forms and deal with Scripture, doctrine, or whatever the preacher wishes to expound upon, a Homily is different. "By means of the homily the mysteries of the faith and the guiding principles of the Christian life are expounded from the sacred text," the *Constitution on the Sacred Liturgy* tells us; the Homily is "part of the liturgy itself" (CSL, 52). Unlike a sermon, a Homily always flows from the liturgy—it depends on "the sacred text," on the Scriptures, the prayers, the liturgical seasons. It is, in short, an integral part of the celebration of the Eucharist, and thus it can be given only by an ordained minister—a bishop, priest, or deacon.

Lay leaders at the children's Liturgy of the Word do not give Homilies. But that does not mean that lay leaders do not preach. Throughout this resource, we use the term "reflection." The reflections lay ministers offer during the children's Liturgy of the Word are certainly preaching in the sense that they explore the readings and help the children apply them to their daily lives. And just like the Homily, a good reflection takes preparation time, a command of Scripture and Church teaching, an ability to speak in an engaging way, and a fair bit of imagination as well.

The *Directory for Masses with Children* refers to the reflection offered during the children's Liturgy of the Word as a Homily (17), but later documents have provided further clarity on this question. The "Introduction" to the *Lectionary for Masses with Children* states that when a priest or deacon is not available to give a Homily, there should still be an "explanation of the Scripture readings" (LMC, 10) by one of the adults present. Many parish communities use the term "reflection" to describe the lay preaching that happens in children's Liturgy of the Word. While this may seem like a matter of semantics, it is an important distinction, reminding us that the Homily is a liturgical act performed by an ordained minister.

PREPARATION

Before the children can express their ideas about the reading's meaning, they need to engage with its content. Depending on the reading, the prayer leader may find that giving the children some background information, such as historical context or the meaning of some new words, might help them to engage with the reading on a deeper level. The prayer leader should also be aware of connections between the different readings for the Sunday, and how the readings relate to the time of the liturgical year.

DIALOGUE

A Homily or reflection can sometimes take the form of a dialogue (see DMC, 48). This might seem strange at first, since Homilies at Mass don't usually involve much spoken input from the congregation. Making the reflection or Homily a more active dialogue in the Liturgy of the Word with children can help the children to stay engaged, though, and is more practical than it would be in the main assembly since the group of children is usually fairly small. These dialogues are intended to help the children to reflect deeply on the Scripture reading and how it relates to their lived experience. The dialogue should never resemble a "quiz" on surface-level details like names or places mentioned in the Scripture reading. If you choose to incorporate dialogue into the reflections, you will want to remain conscious that the *Directory for Masses with Children* recommends this practice "sometimes," not all of the time. You will want to maintain balance between reflections that incorporate a lot of dialogue, reflections that incorporate just a little dialogue, and reflections that involve no dialogue at all.

A dialogue about a Scripture reading might go as follows:

PRAYER LEADER: What happened in today's Gospel Reading?

CHILD: Jesus and Peter were talking.

PRAYER LEADER: What were they talking about?

CHILD: Jesus asked Peter if he loved him.

PRAYER LEADER: Hmmm. Don't you think Jesus already knew that Peter loved him?

CHILDREN: [*They nod.*]

PRAYER LEADER: Well, then, I wonder why he asked him.

CHILD: Peter acted like he didn't know Jesus before he died. That wasn't very nice.

PRAYER LEADER: I wonder why Peter acted like he didn't know Jesus.

CHILD: Maybe he was scared that the people who were hurting Jesus would hurt him, too.

PRAYER LEADER: Hmmm. So now Peter is seeing Jesus again, after he acted like he didn't know him, and Jesus asks him if he loves him. Can anyone remember how many times Jesus asked?

CHILD: Three.

PRAYER LEADER: I wonder why he asked so many times.

CHILD: He said he didn't know him three times, too, right?

PRAYER LEADER: Yes. [*Pause.*] I wonder how Peter felt when he was talking to Jesus.

CHILDREN: Sad . . . Embarrassed . . . Ashamed . . . Mad at himself.

PRAYER LEADER: Jesus was Peter's friend, and Peter let him down. I wonder if any of you have ever felt let down by a friend.

[*A few children may tell stories about times when they felt let down by their friends. The prayer leader encourages the children to tell how it made them feel when their friends let them down.*]

PRAYER LEADER: Did Jesus forgive Peter?

CHILDREN: Yes.

PRAYER LEADER: I wonder why.

CHILD: Because he loved him.

PRAYER LEADER: Even after he did such a bad thing to Jesus?

CHILDREN: Yes.

PRAYER LEADER: I wonder what we can do when our friends let us down.

CHILD: We can forgive them.

PRAYER LEADER: I wonder what we should do if we let one of our friends down.

CHILD: We should say sorry.

PRAYER LEADER: I wonder what Jesus does for us when we let him down.

CHILD: He forgives us.

The prayer leader can bring the conversation to a close by talking about how Jesus always loves us and is ready to forgive us, and how we are called to love and forgive one another.

GUIDED REFLECTION

One of the Church's oldest forms of prayer is a process of reflecting on Scripture called *lectio divina*, or "divine reading." This is a process in which someone reads a piece of Scripture several times in a row, meditating upon it in different ways in order to come to a deep experience of God. Sometimes, you might take inspiration from this practice and choose to proclaim a short reading more than once to the children, encouraging them to focus on different aspects of it each time you read it. For example, if you were reading the story of the Prodigal Son, you might invite the children to reflect on the story from the perspective of the father as you read it the first time, and then from the perspective of the younger son as you read it the second time. This helps the children to consider the reading from multiple perspectives, and shows them how we can interact with Scripture internally by reflecting on it in our hearts and minds.

ACTING OUT THE READING

Some parishes try to make the Scripture more engaging to the children by involving them in acting out the Scripture story like a play, for example, similar to how we proclaim the Gospel in the main assembly on Palm Sunday. The documents recommend that this be done sparingly, if at all, in the proclamation of the Word itself. The individual readings may be divided among more than one reader, so long as the readers are well-prepared, but the majority of the children should be listening rather than proclaiming. Costumes and sets should never be used for the proclamation of the Word during children's Liturgy of the Word.

> The Mass is not a historical reenactment of the events of salvation history and care should be taken not to give the impression that the liturgy of the word is a play.
>
> "Introduction," *Lectionary for Masses with Children*, 52

Writing the Prayer of the Faithful

ABOUT THE PRAYER OF THE FAITHFUL

The Prayer of the Faith marks the conclusion of the Liturgy of the Word. It does not simply come after the readings: this prayer flows from the living Word of God, at work in the hearts of all gathered, teaching them, inspiring them, renewing them. Having listened to the Word of God, having reflected on the readings in the Homily or reflection, we pray to God with intercessions for the Church to whom Christ entrusted the Gospel, and for the world to which we are commissioned to bring the Gospel. The Prayer of the Faithful acts as a hinge, a bridge, between the two parts of the Mass—it leads us from the Table of the Word of God to the Table of the Eucharist.

The Prayer of the Faithful is intended to change every time the Mass is celebrated. Indeed, it can hardly fulfill its function unless it does. Each community is encouraged to compose their own Prayer of the Faithful. The petitions are not to be written carelessly or hastily, nor should they be overextended in number or length. The *General Instruction of the Roman Missal* provides the criteria for which these prayers are to be written (see GIRM, 70).

In the intercessions we pray for:

⊙ The needs of the Church

⊙ Public authorities and the salvation of the whole world

⊙ Those burdened by any kind of difficulty

⊙ The local community

THE PARTS OF THE PRAYER OF THE FAITHFUL

The Prayer of the faithful should include:

INTRODUCTORY COMMENT: This is something that the prayer leader will say to introduce the intercessions. The introductory comment is always addressed to the people, not to God or Jesus, since it is the prayer leader's (or in the case of Mass, the priest's) invitation to them to engage their priestly function of offering prayer. Think of it as a statement. For example, the prayer leader might say: *Jesus came to bring us salvation, and he has promised to come again. As we await his coming, we pray.*

INTERCESSIONS: The intercessions or petitions express the needs of the Church, the world, the oppressed, and the local community. The petitions are "general" and not particular. Here is an example: *For all who are struggling with the challenges of illness, especially Jane, Roger, Margaret, Gene, and Andrew: May God's healing presence be in their lives.* This prayer is general because it prays for all people struggling with illness, but then includes particular names rather than only including particular names. For example, a prayer that is not general would look like this: *For Jane, Roger, Margaret, Gene, and Andrew who are struggling with illness: May God's healing presence be in their lives.* The former, more general prayer, is the most appropriate for liturgical prayer. While the community is concerned about one person, the community's task is to pray for all and on behalf of all. Intercessory prayer "knows no boundaries and extends to one's enemies (CCC, 2647).

Usually, the intercessions follow the same basic format. We may begin with the word "For" and end with the words, "we pray." We start out by naming the specific situation, and then expand upon it to make it more general. Here are a few more examples:

For all of the people in California whose homes were destroyed in the forest fires this week, and for all victims of natural disasters, we pray:

For Allison's grandmother and for all those who have died, we pray:

Here are some tips to help compose the particular petitions.

1. The Church
   - ◉ Are there words or phrases from the Scriptures that can be used?

   - ◉ What things do you think the pope might be worried about right now? How should we pray for him and for all those who serve the Church?

2. The World
   - ◉ Are there words or phrases from the Scriptures that can be used?

   - ◉ What big stories have you read about our president or the leaders of other nations in the news lately?

   - ◉ What difficulties do you think our president or the leaders of other nations might be facing right now?

3. The Oppressed
   - ◉ Are there words or phrases from the Scriptures that can be used?

   - ◉ When have you seen the suffering of human beings? What happened?

   - ◉ What have you seen in the news about people suffering this week?

4. The Local Community
   - ◉ Are there words or phrases from the Scriptures that can be used?

   - ◉ What needs have you seen in your parish, school, religious education program, your neighborhood, or city? Is there anything "big" going on right now?

   - ◉ Do you know anyone who is sick?

⊙ Do you know any families who are mourning
   the loss of a loved one?

When we pray for the local community, we often include those who are sick
or for those who have died. It is best that you not lump together the names
of the sick and the names of the dead into one intercession, as this can lead
children to believe that those are sick are going to die.

CHILDREN'S RESPONSE: Often, we respond to the intercessions by saying,
"Lord, hear our prayer." This is a good response to use with children since it
is widely used and easy to remember. Sometimes, writers of intercessions try
to vary the acclamation. While permissible, this often results in confusion
since the traditional response becomes an ingrained part of the ritual. Usually, it is best practice to go with whatever is ordinarily used in your parish.

CONCLUDING PRAYER: The Prayer of the Faithful concludes with a short
prayer. Write this prayer by following this format: "You, Who, Do, Through."

Use this format for the closing prayer:

1. **YOU:** Name God the Father (for example, "God of mercy, . . .")

2. **WHO:** Tell what God does. What is the quality of God you are
appealing to? What did you hear in the Scripture readings about God?
(For example, "you sent us the gift of your Son.")

3. **DO:** Make this an action statement. What do you want God
to do? In this case, we usually want him to hear our prayers. (For example,
"Hear our prayers and grant them if it is your will.")

4. **THROUGH:** Conclude with the words, "Through Christ our Lord.
Amen."

   If needed, remember to have the Prayer of the Faithful reviewed by your
pastor or liturgist or other appropriate staff member in time to have it ready to
go before the liturgy. If a volunteer minister is reading the prayers you might
send it to them ahead of time so that they can prepare.

Interacting with the Children

CHANNELING THE CHILDREN'S ENERGY

Sometimes, the children may become so wound-up that it can be hard to recapture their attention. In these times, asking them for a moment of silence, as they recall that God is in their midst, usually helps. At other times, the children

Allow children time to think about your question and provide time for them to answer.

may be eerily quiet in response to your questions. In these moments, allow the children to think for a few moments about the questions that you have posed. Remember that silence does not necessarily mean that the children are bored or do not understand. Silence can mean that the children are thoughtful. Avoid the temptation to stop the period of silence by stepping in too quickly with answers. Allow the children some time to simply be with the question.

WHAT HAPPENS WHEN YOU DON'T KNOW THE ANSWER?

Relax! You and the children are engaged together in a process of listening to God's Word and exploring what it reveals in your hearts. Listening to God's Word and wondering about its meaning for you is a lifelong process, and you won't ever have all of the answers.

When the children ask you questions and you don't know the answers, you will want to handle them differently depending on the type of question. If the children ask you a factual question with a clear answer, like "Who is St. Luke?" then you can tell them that you don't know, but that you will find out and will tell them next time. Follow

Ask questions and be affirming of the children's answers.

through with an answer the next time you gather with the children.

If the children ask you a question that does not have an obvious answer, like "Why does God let people die?" then this is an opportunity for you and the children to wonder about God together. You might say, "That is a good question. What do you think? What do the other children in this room think?" Affirm the children's ideas by saying things like, "That is an interesting idea," gently redirecting them if they go too far afield. You will want to hold back from offering your opinion before soliciting the children's ideas. If you give your opinion first, the children may be less likely to offer ideas of their own, thinking that the leader's thought must be correct.

DEALING WITH DISCIPLINE ISSUES, WORRISOME COMMENTS, OR INAPPROPRIATE COMMENTS

The Liturgy of the Word with children is best suited for those who wish to be there, and a child who does not want to be there can be a major distraction to the other children and a big challenge for the prayer leader. It is a good idea to have at least one assistant whose job is "crowd control." This person should quietly approach a child whose behavior is distracting others while the prayer leader continues with the celebration of the Word. If children are talking to one another or physically engaging with one another, they will need to be separated. If a child continues to be disruptive even when separated from the others, he or she may need to leave the group and return to his or her parents in the main assembly. If a certain child's behavior is an ongoing problem, then a consultation with his or her parents is in order. Depending on your parish's approach, this can be done by the individual prayer leader, or by the person who is in charge of coordinating the leaders of the Liturgy of the Word with children. If parents would like to join their children in the celebration of the Liturgy of the Word to assist with any behavior issues, you can consider that option.

You will want to establish an open line of communication with parents of children who partake in the Liturgy of the Word with children so that you can easily communicate with them if discipline issues do arise. There are two types of issues requiring parental involvement that commonly arise in the Liturgy of the Word with children: misbehavior and worrisome comments. When children misbehave, perhaps by talking, acting out, annoying others, and so on, you may need to return them to their parents in the main assembly before the end of the Liturgy of the Word. If there is an ongoing issue with a child, the parents should be consulted so that they can be part of the solution. Some children may also make worrisome comments during the Liturgy of the Word, such as, "When my mom and dad fight, it scares me." Do not draw attention to the child's comment during the Liturgy of the Word, but do raise it later with parents so that they are aware. If something about a child's comments or demeanor leave you with the uneasy sense that the child may have been emotionally, physically, or sexually abused, then it is important that you communicate your concerns to someone in authority, such as your parish's director of religious education or your pastor. Your diocese's training for working with children may have included some information on what to do if you suspect abuse. If so, then you should follow your diocesan guidelines in reporting your concerns.

Frequently Asked Questions

1. What is a prayer leader?

This resource deliberately refers to those who lead the Liturgy of the Word with children as prayer leaders—not as catechists, teachers, or facilitators. This is because the goal of the leader of children's Liturgy of the Word is quite different from that of the catechist: the goal is not to teach doctrine but to lead prayer. The prayer leader does not explain the Scripture readings; rather, he or she breaks open the Word with the children. The prayer leader is not focused on teaching but on being a channel of God's Word, accompanying the children on their faith journey, listening to them, and helping them share their own experiences of God's presence in their lives.

The lay prayer leader is not a homilist, giving a "little Homily" for the little ones. The prayer leader does not prepare a Homily; rather, he or she prepares to help the Scriptures come to life as the children join in conversation about them. Essentially, the prayer leader's job is to ask the right questions and let the children lead the way. We believe that the Holy Spirit is active in the liturgical moments when the children share their experiences of God. When the children are sharing their experience of the Word in their lives, the "rightness" of the children's answers should not be the prayer leader's first concern. Rather, the prayer leader takes on an attitude of affirmation and wonder at the children's responses, and gently guides a holy conversation in which the children begin to discover for themselves how the Scriptures can illuminate or change their lives.

In addition to leading the reflection time, the prayer leader has other responsibilities as well: to lead the children in liturgical prayer, including some of the dialogues and prayers of the Mass as well as in the Prayer of the Faithful. Like the priest and deacon during the Mass, the prayer leader needs to lead these prayers with warmth but also with dignity, gently commanding and holding attention, both when speaking and when leading the children in the silent prayer that is also part of the liturgy.

2.   Who can be a prayer leader?

Anyone who wishes to help children in their growth as disciples of Christ and to promote their love for God can lead the Liturgy of the Word with children—priests, deacons, and laypeople. People who are gifted with the ability to communicate well with children will do a great service by taking on this role. One does not need to be a parent to engage in this ministry. You should like children and be comfortable speaking with them. Prayer leaders should have their own ongoing relationships with God, and should be eager to help children in their relationships with God. Being an effective prayer leader starts with being a practicing Catholic, active in the life of the parish, living and loving the Catholic faith. Leading prayer with children makes additional demands. You need to be an effective communicator to grab and hold the attention of young people. You need to be able to express complex ideas in simple language. You need to be patient. You need to be able to live with a bit of chaos, a bit of noise in the background. You do not necessarily need to be a parent, but you need to be comfortable connecting with children of various ages. Older teens may serve as prayer leaders if they meet all of the necessary requirements.

In addition to the training you will receive from your parish to be a prayer leader, every adult involved in the Liturgy of the Word with children, from the leader, to the cantor, to the assistant, should undergo all mandatory background screening and training in the protection of children, as required by your diocese. It may seem as though it is unnecessary since prayer leaders are unlikely to ever be alone with a single child. It is still vital, though, because when children see someone as an authority figure, they are likely to trust that person and follow that person's guidance. Criminal background checks might uncover information about a person that would otherwise go undetected. Diocesan policies should always be followed completely in this regard, with no exceptions. Your parish staff will coordinate this training with you.

3.   Is the Liturgy of the Word with children the same as religious education classes?

Although the overall message may be similar, the Liturgy of the Word with children and religious instruction are very different. The Liturgy of the Word with children is a part of the Mass. While we do learn things by participating in the Mass, particularly through the Homily, the primary intention of the Mass is for the faithful to gather together and praise God. The Liturgy of the Word with children is about helping children to hear the Word of God in a way that makes sense to them and bears reference to their lives, and allowing that Word to speak to them in their hearts. It is not necessarily about cognitive learning. The "Introduction" to the *Lectionary for Masses with Children* tells us: "The liturgy of the word is neither a catechetical session nor an introduction to biblical history. The liturgy celebrates the word of God in narrative and song, makes it visible in gesture and symbol and culminates in the celebration of the eucharist" (LMC, 24).

The Liturgy of the Word with children is intended to take place in a space readied for worship, while religious education classes typically take place in a classroom. Religious education courses are oriented toward an overall curriculum that may include Scripture, but this is not its primary focus. The Liturgy of the Word with children is not curriculum—it is liturgical prayer. As prayer, it is always oriented toward the Sunday Scripture readings, and it requires that the prayer leader breaks open the Scripture with the children so that they may experience an ongoing conversion and deepen their relationship with God.

The Liturgy of the Word with children should never be a replacement for religious education classes; used as a babysitting service; as a "time out," or place for children who are restless or acting out in church; or as playtime (although it does not always have to be serious).

4.   What is the difference between a Lectionary and a Bible? Isn't the Scripture the same? Can't I use the Bible instead?

The Lectionary and the Bible are not the same. The Bible contains the revealed Word of God in its entirety, the Old and New Testaments. The Lectionary is a liturgical book which includes adapted selections from the Bible arranged according to the liturgical year. These readings—drawn from both the Old and the New Testaments—are short passages (sometimes called *pericopes*, a Greek word meaning extract or selection) intended to be proclaimed aloud during public worship. The Lectionary juxtaposes readings from different parts of the Bible in order to give us insights into the meaning of the feasts and seasons of the liturgical year. It is "an arrangement of biblical readings that provides the faithful with a knowledge of the whole of God's word, in a pattern suited to the purpose. Throughout the liturgical year . . . the choice and sequence of readings are aimed at giving Christ's faithful an ever-deepening perception of the faith they profess and of the history of salvation" ("Introduction," to the *Lectionary for Mass*, 60).

The Lectionary includes almost all of the New Testament, and a good portion of the Old Testament, but it is not a substitute for the Bible, the revealed Word of God. Rather, by pondering the readings of the Mass, we should grow in love of the Scriptures, and read them, meditate on them, and study them in the Bible.

Neither the Lectionary nor the Bible is carried in the entrance procession (see GIRM, 120d)—that is reserved to the *Book of the Gospels*. The Lectionary is simply placed at the ambo before the liturgy begins. An additional Lectionary that will be used for children's Liturgy of the Word should also be placed in a convenient location before the liturgy begins. It should be easily accessible so that the priest celebrant may present it to the prayer leader before the children are dismissed (see pages 8–10).

The *Directory for Masses with Children* says that if all the readings assigned to the day seem unsuited "to the capacity of children" (DMC, 43) it is permissible to choose other readings either from the Lectionary or directly from the Bible, but taking into account the liturgical season.

Even though the *Directory* presents the Bible as an option, utilizing this option should be considered very carefully and always in discussion with your pastor or liturgist. One problem with this option is that reading out loud from a Bible can be clumsy—it can be easy to lose your place, and it might be difficult for your listeners to tell what is going on unless you identify pronouns or add a few details to the passage. For instance, you might need to inform everyone that Moses is standing on Mount Sinai when all of this happens, or that Jesus is speaking these words you are about to say. The Lectionary already includes these adjustments.

It is important to know that when the *Directory for Masses with Children* was published or promulgated (mandated for liturgical use by the Vatican) this was before the *Lectionary for Masses with Children* was published. The *Directory for Masses with Children* recommended that Conferences of Bishops create and publish a Lectionary adapted for children. Because this has happened since the *Directory* was published it is probably not a good idea or best practice to use the Bible. The adaptation has already been done for you. The *Lectionary for Masses with Children*, of course, is filled with readings suited "to the capacity of the children" (DMC, 43).

5. The *Lectionary for Mass* is based on the *New American Bible*. And the *Lectionary for Masses with Children* has been adapted for the needs of children. Is this adaptation a paraphrase of the NAB? Is it a different translation? Is this approved to use in ritual?

There are many translations of Scripture. The translation for the standard Lectionary is based on the *New American Bible* (NAB). The translation of Scripture used in the *Lectionary for Masses with Children* is called the *Contemporary English Version*. The *Contemporary English Version* is not a paraphrase of the Bible but a translation from the original languages.

A newer translation based on the *New American Bible* has been completed and approved by the United States Conference of Catholic Bishops. This translation has been submitted to the Vatican for approval. At the time of this printing, approval (*recognitio*) of this new translation has not been granted. Until this approval is received, you can still use the ritual book that is currently in print and available from Catholic Book Publishing. This book uses the *Contemporary English Version* of the Bible.

6. The Lectionary has page numbers, but it also has numbers in the corners. What are these numbers?

These are Lectionary numbers. They are shorthand to help someone refer to sets of readings. For instance, in the children's Lectionary the number for the readings for the First Sunday of Lent in Year A is 18. In Year B it is 19. And in Year C it is 20.

In the standard Lectionary, the number for the First Sunday of Lent is 22. So the numbers in the children's Lectionary do not match the numbers in the regular Lectionary.

You will not, of course, find every Lectionary number in each volume of the children's Lectionary. For instance, the volume for Sundays in Year A has numbers 1, 4, 7, and so on. Year B has 2, 5, 8, and so on. Year C has 3, 6, 9, and so on. In all the volumes, the Lectionary numbers increase from front to back, as you would expect.

7. Are there times when I am obligated to use the *Lectionary for Masses with Children* and not the standard Lectionary?

In one word, no. In fact, ordinarily you would use the standard Lectionary if the readings seem suited to the comprehension of the people gathered for Mass.

Whether or not to use the *Lectionary for Masses with Children* is a necessary judgment call. On the one hand, children are being introduced to the Scriptures, and the *Lectionary for Mass* was prepared to open up the richness of the Bible. On the other hand, the liturgy requires participation, and comprehension helps that happen.

The *Lectionary for Masses with Children* was prepared to help children better comprehend the Scripture readings. It also was prepared, in its own words, because "the Church intends to lead [children] into one community of faith, formed by the proclamation of the word of God" (LMC, 12). In other words, the *Lectionary for Masses with Children* is meant to enable children to become active participants in parish worship.

8. At what age should children attend a separate Liturgy of the Word?

The Liturgy of the Word with children tends to be most effective for children who are about five to nine years of age. The *Directory for Masses with Children* states that it is for children who have "not yet entered the period of preadolescence" (DMC, 6), and the "Introduction" to the *Lectionary for Masses with Children* tells us that it is for "children of elementary grades" (LMC, 15). Children of this age can listen attentively to Scripture and respond to questions about what happens in the readings. They can also learn simple responses to the readings or prayers.

Children younger than five years of age are often confused by the direction of conversations or the purposes of questions. You may find that, sometimes, they respond with answers that don't seem to be on the same wavelength as those of the older children.

Children who are older than ten, on the other hand, are often able to comprehend the priest's Homily. Usually, a child of this age should be able to participate in Mass alongside the rest of the parish community. If an older child or teen has severe cognitive limitations, however, some thought should be given to whether he or she might benefit from the Liturgy of the Word with children. The *Directory for Masses with Children* emphasizes that it primarily concerns pre-adolescent children, that it "does not speak directly of children who are physically or mentally handicapped, because a broader adaptation is sometimes necessary for them," but that "the following norms may also be applied to the handicapped, with the necessary changes" (DMC, 6).

9. What resources will I need to lead prayer?

The Lectionary is the best place to start your preparation. A careful and prayerful reading of the Scriptures during the week leading up to Sunday will open you to the many ways in which the Liturgy of the Word is intimately connected to the entire liturgical celebration. See pages 28–33 in this resource about using the Lectionary.

Regarding other resources, many Catholic publishers have published materials that can be used to help the leader to understand the readings for a particular Sunday and to facilitate the Homily or reflection with the children. You will want to review several of the resources on the market and decide which is best for your situation. Keep in mind that the Liturgy of the Word with children is not intended to be instruction time, craft time, or playtime. You will find that most catechetical resources, and even some resources intended specifically for the Liturgy of the Word with children, are primarily comprised of crafts and activity pages and do not include any liturgical material or material for a Homily or reflection. You may want to avoid or heavily adapt these resources in order to ensure that the children experience the Liturgy of the Word as a prayerful and reflective experience rather than as a school or play experience. It is recommended that you reflect with the children on the Word by talking with them in the Homily or reflection, rather than by handing out worksheets or activities, in order to prepare them to listen carefully to the Homily in the main assembly one day. Refer to the list of resources that are provided in this booklet on pages 53–56.

10. How are parents involved?

Regardless of their level of involvement in the Liturgy of the Word with children at your parish, parents are a vital part of your work with the children. *Lumen gentium* (LG), a document of the Second Vatican Council, speaks of the importance of parents in the religious upbringing of their children: "In what might be regarded as the domestic church, the parents are to be the first preachers of the faith for their children by word and example" (LG, 11). The "Introduction" to the *Lectionary for Masses with Children* reinforces this idea: "the Church . . . seeks to protect and foster the domestic church which is the Christian family" (LMC, 14; referencing DMC, 16). The allowance for children's Liturgy of the Word isn't about giving parents a break, it is about helping them with their very important role. When children engage with the Word of God at Mass in a way that helps them to understand the Scripture and apply it to their lives, that makes the work that parents, teachers, and catechists do more fruitful.

Parents participate in the Liturgy of the Word by:

- ◉ Encouraging their children to attend, but never forcing or bribing them to do so

- Emphasizing that the Liturgy of the Word with children is part of Mass, and should be taken seriously

- Engaging their children in conversations about the Sunday Scripture

- Helping their children to live out the Sunday Scripture in their daily lives

- Working with leaders of the Liturgy of the Word with children to address any discipline problems that may arise

- Reinforcing the importance of prayer and Mass attendance in all aspects of family life at home

Your parish staff should communicate the guidelines and practices for the Liturgy of the Word with children. As a prayer leader, you should be conscious of discipline issues and of materials to send home (see page 43). You will be able to address questions about the nature of children's Liturgy of the Word but you should always feel comfortable to direct major questions to your parish staff.

11. Can I send material home with the children?

You may want to consider sending some material home in order to help parents reflect with their children on what they heard in the Scriptures. You should avoid, if at all possible, having the children carry materials back with them into the main assembly when the Liturgy of the Word has concluded, since these materials can serve as distractions and may give children the impression that the Mass is over. Instead, see if you can hand out these materials at the end of Mass as people are leaving, or if you can disseminate them on the parish website or through the bulletin. You should always consult with your pastor, liturgist, director of religious education, or other staff member before giving out materials.

Resources

PREPARING THE LITURGY OF THE WORD WITH CHILDREN

The following resources will help prayer leaders understand the nature of Catholic liturgy and facilitate and prepare this prayer with children.

Children's Liturgy of the Word: A Weekly Resource. Chicago, IL: Liturgy Training Publications (annual). This resource contains dismissal texts, the full text of an age-appropriate Homily/reflection, music suggestions, and all of the prayers needed to facilitate a liturgically sound, prayerful celebration of the Liturgy of the Word with children. It is published annually so that the materials are new each year, and is calendar-dated for ease of use.

Sourcebook for Sundays, Seasons, and Weekdays. Chicago, IL: Liturgy Training Publications (annual). An annual pastoral resource that provides information about the seasons, the readings and prayers of the day, as well as ideas for how to celebrate the Liturgy of the Word for children. A great tool for familiarizing yourself with Catholic liturgy.

Piercy, Robert W. *Preparing Masses with Children: 15 Easy Steps.* Chicago, IL: Liturgy Training Publications, 2012. This book gives even the most inexperienced prayer leaders, teachers, and catechists the tools that they need to communicate with principals, pastors, liturgists, and music directors in order to prepare liturgies that are both effective and liturgically sound. Although this book is focused on preparing the entire Mass, the sections on the Liturgy of the Word are relevant and extremely helpful to those who lead the Liturgy of the Word with children.

Walker, Chistopher, and Paule Freeburg. *Music for Children's Liturgy of the Word (Years A, B, and C).* Portland, OR: Oregon Catholic Press, 2001. This series of resources

53

includes the Responsorial Psalm and Gospel Acclamations appropriate for use with children for every Sunday and major feast day of the year.

SCRIPTURE, HOMILY, AND REFLECTION RESOURCES

A prayer leader should familiarize themselves with the Sunday Scriptures and read through commentaries about the Word of God.

At Home with the Word. Chicago, IL: Liturgy Training Publications (annual). This book includes the texts of the Sunday readings for the particular year (Year A, B, or C) with Scripture reflections with questions for study and discussion. A perfect resource for reflecting more on the readings for Sunday.

The Daily Mass Readings: A Simple Reference Guide. Chicago, IL: Liturgy Training Publications (annual). This handy booklet is published annually and provides the citations for the Mass readings for each day of the year. All you need to do is look up the date and you will be able to find the list of readings for Mass.

Lectionary for Masses with Children. Totowa, NJ: Catholic Book Publishing, 2013. The Sunday ritual edition of the Lectionary for Masses with Children, which was out of print for some time, is now (at the time of printing) back in print with Catholic Book Publishing.

Lectionary for Mass: Sundays, Solemnities, Feasts of the Lord and the Saints, Study Edition. Chicago, IL: Liturgy Training Publications, 1999. This convenient and comprehensive paperback volume includes all of the readings for the Sundays of Years A, B, and C and for solemnities and feasts for the dioceses of the United States of America.

Prendergast, Michael R., Susan E. Meyers, and Timothy M. Milinovich. *Pronunciation Guide for the Lectionary: A Comprehensive Resource for Proclaimers of the Word.* Chicago, IL: Liturgy Training Publications, 2009. This is a straightforward pronunciation guide that those who read the Scripture at Mass should have at home when they are preparing for their ministry. Questionable or difficult words from the Lectionary are provided with a simple pronunciation key.

PRAYER AND SPIRITUAL FORMATION

A prayer leader should first and foremost be a person of prayer. Their ongoing personal spiritual formation is important.

Daily Prayer. Chicago, IL: Liturgy Training Publications (annual). This annual resource provides an order of prayer for each day of the liturgical year. Using a familiar order of prayer, it enables further reflection on the sacred mysteries celebrated in the liturgy. The Gospel of the day from the daily Mass is provided, and the prayer texts and reflections are in tune with the observance of the seasons, solemnities, feasts of the Lord, and commemoration of saints celebrated during the liturgical year.

Sunday Prayer for Catechists. Chicago, IL: Liturgy Training Publications (annual). This little prayer book invites catechists, teachers, and all who work with children to develop a habit of personal prayer and to reflect on the Word of God. This annual resource provides Gospel texts from the Sunday Lectionary and reflections that connect the message of Scripture to work with young people in order to help teachers or prayer leaders to grow spiritually through their ministry.

Sunday Prayer for Catholics. Chicago, IL: Liturgy Training Publications (annual). This book follows the liturgical year and provides the Gospel and a reflection for each Sunday. Its portable size allows you to easily slip it into a purse, briefcase, or backpack so you'll always have the Gospel with reflections readily available. This booklet is an aid to help you nourish your faith through the week as you prepare for Sunday.

LITURGICAL DOCUMENTS

Leaders of the Liturgy of the Word with children should have some familiarity with the following documents. A brief summary of each of these documents follows. Full texts of many of these documents are found in LTP's liturgy document series, *The Liturgy Documents*. Of course, there are other documents which are valuable and important to read. The documents below are merely a starting point. If you're curious about what other documents to read, your liturgist or pastor will be happy to provide you with this information.

Constitution on the Sacred Liturgy (1963). This is the first document of the Second Vatican Council and provides the theological foundation and pastoral principles for the celebration of all liturgy. These principles also guide the celebration of the separate Liturgy of the Word with children. The themes found throughout this document are indispensable for our understanding of the centrality of the Paschal Mystery, the prominence of God's Word, active participation, adaptation, music, the liturgical year, and liturgical art and architecture. It is from this document that subsequent liturgical documents flow. You can find this document online or in *The Liturgy Documents, Volume One: Fifth Edition* published by Liturgy Training Publications.

The General Instruction of the Roman Missal (2011). This document serves as the introduction to *The Roman Missal*, the ritual book the priest uses to celebrate the Mass. This document provides a comprehensive understanding of what we are doing when we celebrate the liturgy, as well as best practices for implementation. Anyone who prepares liturgy—priests, deacons, liturgists, musicians, catechists, and so on—should be very familiar with its contents. It is essential for leaders of the Liturgy of the Word with children to be familiar with the *General Instruction of the Roman Missal*, especially the second chapter, "The Structure of the Mass, Its Elements, and Its Parts." It is indispensable, even in the Liturgy of the Word with children, to adhere to the principles that guide the prayer of the Church. This document is found at the front of *The Roman Missal* or in *The Liturgy Documents, Volume One: Fifth Edition* published by Liturgy Training Publications.

Directory for Masses with Children (1973). After many years of consultation, the Congregation for Divine Worship and the Discipline of the Sacraments (an office in Rome concerned with the implementation of the liturgy) issued the *Directory for Masses with Children* in 1973. This document was inspired by the work of the Second Vatican Council. It was designed to serve as a supplement to the *General Instruction of the Roman Missal*. With special emphasis on the important connection between liturgy and Christian identity, this directory aimed to lead pre-adolescent children to a better participation with the adult assembly. This document is available in *The Liturgy Documents, Volume Two: Second Edition* published by Liturgy Training Publications.

Lectionary for Mass: Introduction (1998). This document serves as the introduction to the standard *Lectionary for Mass*. It provides theological reflection on the connection between Scripture and the liturgy, the structure of the Liturgy of the Word, the ministers of the Liturgy of the Word, the nature of the Homily, and instructions for how to celebrate the Liturgy of the Word properly. This document is found at the beginning of the Lectionary or in *The Liturgy Documents, Volume One: Fifth Edition* published by Liturgy Training Publications.

Lectionary for Masses with Children: Introduction (1992). This document serves as the introduction to the *Lectionary for Masses with Children*. It is found in each volume of the LMC. This introduction explains the nature of the Liturgy of the Word, the purpose of the adapted readings, and how to celebrate properly.

ONLINE RESOURCES

How to Use the Children's Lectionary
National Pastoral Musicians
www.npm.org/Sections/images/Children's%20Lectionary.pdf
A wonderful article helping prayer leaders navigate the *Lectionary for Masses with Children*.

Today's Liturgy with Children
Oregon Catholic Press
www.ocp.org/articles/series/todays_liturgy_children
A series of articles regarding reflections, Scripture commentaries, and singing with children.

Glossary

ACCLAMATIONS: An exclamation (of joy) by the assembly during worship. Certain responses of the assembly are classified as acclamations, as opposed to hymns, responses, or other literary forms. "Amen" is an example of an acclamation, whereas the Gloria is a hymn and the Lamb of God is a series of invocations in the style of a litany.

AMBO: A dignified and stationary place from which the readings, Responsorial Psalm, and the Gospel are proclaimed. It may be used for giving the Homily and for announcing the intentions of the Prayer of the Faithful.

COLLECT: The opening prayer of the Mass. It sums up or "collects" all the thoughts and prayers of the assembly, and concludes the Introductory Rites. After the Collect, everyone is seated and the Liturgy of the Word begins.

CONCLUDING RITES: The last part of the Mass, following the Communion Rite. It begins immediately after the Prayer after Communion and consists of brief announcements, a greeting, a blessing, and the dismissal of the assembly.

CONSTITUTION ON THE SACRED LITURGY: The first document of the Second Vatican Council, also known by its Latin title *Sacrosanctum Concilium*. It was promulgated on December 4, 1963 and, in particular, allowed the celebration of liturgical rites in the vernacular, called for the active participation of the assembly, and ordered the revision of all liturgical rites.

CREED: The formula that expresses what the Church believes about God. It is also referred to as the Symbol or the Profession of Faith. At Mass, if required, the Profession of Faith occurs after the Homily, and it usually takes the form of the Niceno-Constantinopolitan Creed, although the Apostles' Creed may also be used, especially at Masses with children.

DIRECTORY FOR MASSES WITH CHILDREN: This document was approved by Pope Paul VI in 1973. It was developed as a response to the direction in the *Constitution on the Sacred Liturgy*, which provided for adaptations of the liturgy for special groups. The *Directory for Masses with Children* is a unique pastoral document focused on the liturgical formation of children.

DISMISSAL: The final, formal invitation by the deacon, or, in his absence, by the priest, for the assembly to go forth from the liturgical celebration. The word can also refer to the dismissal of the catechumens after the Homily at Mass and the dismissal of children to a separate Liturgy of the Word after the Collect.

FIRST READING: The first Scripture reading during the Liturgy of the Word. On Sundays and other important days, it is usually taken from the Old Testament, or, during Easter Time, from the Acts of the Apostles or Revelation. On weekdays, it may be taken either from the Old Testament or from the New Testament writings of the Apostles, but not from the Gospel accounts.

GENERAL DIRECTORY FOR CATECHESIS: This document replaces an earlier document, *General Catechetical Directory*, published by the Congregation for the Clergy in 1971. The newer document (1997), also from the Congregation for the Clergy, provides theological and pastoral principles for catechesis.

GENERAL INSTRUCTION OF THE ROMAN MISSAL: The document that explains the theological background and gives the directions (or rubrics) for celebrating the Mass. It is a foundational document for anyone involved in the preparation or celebration of the Mass. It appears at the beginning of *The Roman Missal*, though it is often published separately as well. It is often referred to by the abbreviation GIRM.

GOSPEL: The "Good News" of Jesus. Usually, "Gospel" refers to one of the four accounts of the life, Death, and Resurrection of Jesus as written by Matthew, Mark, Luke, and John and found in the Bible. A passage from one of the four accounts of the Gospels is proclaimed at Mass as the last of the readings from Sacred Scripture.

GOSPEL ACCLAMATION: The acclamation that prepares the assembly for the proclamation of the Gospel reading. Usually the Alleluia is sung as the Gospel Acclamation, except during Lent, when it is replaced by other words of praise (for example, "Praise to you, Lord Jesus Christ, King of endless glory").

HOMILY: A breaking open or exhortative explanation of the Scripture readings or of the liturgical day being celebrated. It usually takes place after the proclamation of the Gospel. It is also a reflection on the implications of Scripture and a challenge to the assembly to conversion and renewal. By canonical definition (see *Code of Canon Law* 767.1) the Homily at Mass is reserved to the ordained. At Mass, the Homily is ordinarily given by the priest celebrant, although it may be entrusted to a concelebrating priest or to the deacon. The Homily is to be distinguished from a sermon or reflection. A Homily is an integral part of the liturgy related to the Scripture readings and/or some other aspect of the liturgy; a sermon is a thematic talk given at a liturgy, but not necessarily integrally related to it as part of the liturgical action.

INTRODUCTORY RITES: The name given to the beginning of Mass or another liturgy. It begins with the entrance of the ministers and concludes with the Collect. It is followed by the Liturgy of the Word. Normally, the Introductory Rites at Mass consist of the entrance song and procession, the veneration of the altar, the Sign of the Cross, the Greeting, the Penitential Act, Rite of Sprinkling of Water, the Gloria and then the Collect.

LECTIONARY FOR MASS: The ritual book including the readings for Mass. It is divided into several volumes, which include the readings for Sundays, Solemnities and Feasts of the Lord, Masses for the weekdays and the saints, as well as rituals such as weddings and funerals.

LECTIONARY FOR MASSES WITH CHILDREN: The ritual book including readings that have been adapted for the liturgical and cognitive needs of children.

LECTIONARY FOR MASSES WITH CHILDREN, INTRODUCTION: Every ritual book includes an introduction (in Latin called *praenotanda*). This document serves as the introduction to the children's Lectionary and provides a theological overview of the Word of God in the liturgy as well as specific directions for celebrating the Liturgy of the Word with children.

LITURGY: From the Greek word, *leitourgia*, which means "a public act" (or "the work of the people") performed for the good of the community. In the Roman Catholic Church, the word is used in reference to any of the official rites of the Church as found in the Roman ritual books. This includes, Mass, the Liturgy of the Hours, services of the Liturgy of the Word, and celebrations of the sacraments and blessings.

LITURGY OF THE EUCHARIST: Begins with the Preparation of the Gifts and includes the Eucharistic Prayer, Communion Rite, and Prayer after Communion, during which the action of the Mass is centered around the altar.

LITURGY OF THE WORD: The part of the Mass from the First Reading through the Prayer of the Faithful during which the action of the Mass is centered around the ambo.

PRIEST CELEBRANT: The priest who officiates or is the primary prayer leader for Mass.

PROCESSION: Any formal movement of one or more persons from one place to another in a liturgy.

PROTECTING GOD'S CHILDREN: A training program, also called VIRTUS (www. virtus.org), for preventing child sexual abuse. All parish ministers who work with children should be properly trained in this or similar programs.

REFLECTION: Explanation of the Scripture readings as given by a layperson. During a regular Mass a lay reflection should not replace the Homily. A Homily is always to be given by an ordained minister—priest or deacon. At a separate Liturgy of the Word with children, a lay minister may give the reflection or explanation of the reading following the Gospel. However, this reflection should not be called a Homily.

RESPONSORIAL PSALM: The psalm follows the First Reading. The psalms were composed as lyrics, and they should be sung when possible. As Scripture it is also proclaimed from the ambo along with the other readings. On some occasions, the "song" that follows the First Reading is a canticle from Scripture rather than a psalm. One example is the *Magnificat*.

RITUAL: A name given to any formalized action. Normally, it refers to special religious activities that have a set structure and order, and employ religious symbols and texts. In general, however, "ritual" can refer to any human activity that marks significant moments through expected and repeated patterns of behavior or rules of actions.

THE ROMAN MISSAL: The ritual book that includes the prayers, rubrics (or directions), and other texts needed by the priest celebrant to preside over the Mass and other sacramental celebrations.

RUBRIC: The directions for celebrating liturgy. They are printed in red text in ritual books. The English word comes from the Latin word *ruber*, which means red.

SECOND READING: On Sundays and certain major celebrations, after the First Reading and the Responsorial Psalm, a Second Reading is proclaimed. It is taken from one of the books of the New Testament other than the Gospel accounts.

UNIVERSAL PRAYER: Name given to the last part of the Liturgy of the Word in the celebration of the Mass. Also called the Prayer of the Faithful or Bidding Prayers (and formerly called the General Intercessions), it consists of an introduction to the people by the priest celebrant, followed by various intentions read by the deacon (or reader or another minister), to which the people make a response (for example, "Lord, hear our prayer"), followed by a concluding prayer said by the celebrant.